Living in A
SYDNEY

Practical Guide

Soo Lee & Biswanath Dutta

FIRST EDITION

Contents

Table of Contents

CHAPTER 1 - BEFORE ARRIVAL 12

What you can prepare before coming 13

CHAPTER 2 – FIRST DAY 21

Weather and climate in Sydney 22

What to wear on arrival 24

Must do - on arrival 27

CHAPTER 3 - FIRST MONTH 30

Where to stay 31

Dedication

This book is dedicated to the earlier generations and original owners of Australia, with gratitude and respect, we honour your legacy and strive for unity and inclusivity.

Acknowledgement

This guide is written for those who are actively seeking migration or have migrated to Australia, including short term or for long term through work or seeking to work from Australia to settle in. The book is intended to empower them with more knowledge that local people possess.

Whilst the details in this book is written with Author's experience living in Sydney, information have been checked and verified through additional research to reflect most recent updates and changes to regulations, which will consistently apply to anyone wishes to migrate and reside in wider NSW region (outside of Sydney).

The information provided in this book that are regulatory in nature are subject to change. Any suggestions including tips and recommendations are provided at reader's disposal and their own discretion.

The information should not be used as an absolute and the only guide to rely on to make any material decisions. The information provided is general and broad in nature, combining research and observations made by the author.

This book is not suitable for those who are seeking guidance for Visa options, Financial or Wealth management through the immigration.

We are not endorsing any products through the website reference links provided in this book. The website reference links are neither owned nor produced originally by the author. These are provided for reader's reference purpose only.

How to navigate this book

This book is divided into 5 main sections: before arrival, the first day, the first month, the first year and the longer term in Sydney Australia.

Inside each section, there are various topics you can choose from to explore. You do not necessarily have to read the book in the listed order of content and feel free to jump around as you wish to know more on a particular subject matter.

To guide your reading, certain sections throughout the contents are marked with 'Important' and 'Tips' indications.

Preface

Congratulations on your decision to come to one of the most beautiful places in the earth, Sydney Australia!

I applaud for your bravery and commitment to explore a new land which will reward you for many years to come. I am so glad you will be joining this wonderful place with us. Welcome to Sydney, mate!

Understanding from our very own experience living in Sydney as immigrants, we are hoping this book will be a great guide for your first-time migration experience to be smoother and easier during your process of settling in Australia. Whether it be for short term or for long term visit, we hope you make the most of your stay in Sydney Australia.

In this edition of book, some of the hacks and tips have been tailored towards specifically those coming to Australia for the first time.

Now, let's explore what to be expected and how to prepare settlement in Sydney, Australia.

Chapter 1 -
Before arrival

WHAT YOU CAN PREPARE BEFORE COMING

Setting up your own bank account

Setting up your own bank account can be helpful if you can do it prior to your coming. Not every bank will offer this service, however, if you want to prepare as much as possible prior to your arrival to Sydney, apply for your bank account online.

Refer to:

- https://www.commbank.com.au/moving-to-australia/banking.html

Once you arrive, complete the application process by visiting the nearest bank branch in person. Bring your digital welcome letter, passport and Tax identification number from your home country or any other country.

Transfer money to Australia bank account

This can be a tricky one. You want to think about most efficient way to transfer your money over to Australia without having to pay transfer fee or too much tax which can be imposed by the country. So check prior to making any arrangements. Of course, you might not be able to transfer it prior to your coming, however, it is good to research digital remittance method before you arrive to Australia.

One option is to transfer money using bank transfer service. Alternative way is to use Multi Currency Card to transfer the money to the designated bank account which you have opened.

You can bring in physical currency. According to RBA (Reserve Bank of Australia), there is no limit to the amount that can be brought into or taken out of Australia. You must, however, declare the amount you bring when it is over $10,000 AUD or more by an individual.

Finding a place to stay

It is important to know where you will be staying in advance. As of 2023, available rooms (vacancy) are low (below 1%) in Sydney Australia. The situation might gradually improve, however, due to high demand for migration to Sydney, price of accommodation can be high.

TIP: Refer to the Where to stay section under Chapter 3 - First one month in this book on how to prepare your accommodation.

Phone roaming from your home country

It is advised that you keep your phone on roaming to stay communicated with family members or any contact in case of emergency.

What to bring and pack

Ethnic / Traditional Clothes

Do try bringing Ethnic wears of your choices and all the other clothes you usually enjoy wearing back at home. Ethnic wears are available in Sydney, however, as it is not common outfit by majority, chances are you will have to pay 5-10 times more the price of what you will pay in your home country for much less quality.

Winter Clothes

These are easily purchasable in Australia and might be better to get them directly while you are staying here as the clothes are adequately designed for Australia's climate.

However, do bring 2-3 pieces of your warmest clothes you have - long sleeve top, jacket, hoodie, long pants just to avoid getting shocked or even becoming sick from not wearing proper attire in case you don't have any.

Socks

Please bring at least 5 pairs. Unless you are coming during summer, your foot will thank you for wearing socks. Again, when you are running low, you get more in Sydney.

Personal belongings

Bring your laptops, mobile phone, musical instruments, and others. The key point here is, bring the items that are not immediately replaceable and personally important to you.

Official Documents

Do make sure to bring all your documents that are issued from government or institutes such as bank to prove your identity and your relationships with your family. Passport, Birth certificate, Marriage certificate, and academic certificate are to name few. Don't leave anything behind.

TIP: Make a digital copy and photocopy scan of each document. Bookmark the folder where you are saving the documents so you can easily access whenever you require it.

Medicines

Do bring your medicines at least 1 month worth, especially your prescribed and important medicines you need to take on regular basis. To continue the medicine in Sydney, you must see visit GP (general practitioners) to buy the medicine from pharmacy with a prescription. GP appointment is necessary most of the time and it is expected that doctors are not available immediately unless emergency. Also, be aware not all the medicines you can get over the counter in your home country may not be equally available in Sydney over the counter as medical practice and regulations are different from each country.

Toiletries

Do bring small sized essentials if possible - toothpaste, brush, shampoo, lotion, cream, shaving cream. These are easy to get but I suggest you bring them at least for 2-3 days just so that your settling is an easy one.

Cash

In Australia, most of financial transactions can be done electronically. There is very less requirement to use cash. However, as you will not have Australian bank account set up as you arrive, do bring spare cash. It is important to note, since the Covid-19 outbreak, a lot of merchants started to not accept cash.

TIP: Arrange an international transaction debit card with 0% transaction fee before coming.

International usage permitted credit card

If you already have international transaction permitted credit card, do bring it. Make sure to check with your provider of credit card to enable to transaction to be made in Australia and any other world (including transit country) prior to the departure. To book a Taxi (or Uber, Didi, Ola) for your arrival, you will require a digital transaction permitted card such as credit card or debit card.

IMPORTANT:

Debit card is also known as cheque card in some countries. Make sure to bring one which is allowed to use overseas upon arrival without having to activate it prior to making the transaction.

What to NOT bring and pack

Raw Ingredients or Unpackaged Foods

Australia immigration rules are strict with foods that are not packaged and sealed. What this means is, coming to Australia with home prepared ingredients or even food from your favourite local shop is not ok, unless they have been properly sealed and packaged. What you can expect on arrival at the Sydney airport, you will most likely have to throw them in the bin before leaving the airport. This may not always apply 100% as immigration officer will check each item, but you are very likely be subjected to this rule.

TIP: Do not pack any food items for your first travel to Australia to avoid any hassle.

Refer to:

- https://www.abf.gov.au/entering-and-leaving-australia/can-you-bring-it-in
- https://www.agriculture.gov.au/biosecurity-trade/travelling/moving-immigrating

Pre-packaged and labelled Food

Speaking of pre-packaged foods, you will find Sydney has plenty of international grocers. Chances are you will find the basic ingredients from your home country easily available in Sydney. Even though you will be very much tempted, don't bring too many packaged food thinking you will not easily get find them in Sydney.

Utensils and cooking processors

Understand that food utensils and cooking processors, such as knife, pots, plates, pressure cooker, blender, and many others are very easy to get at a reasonable price in Australia. Remind you, you will be protected by Australian consumer law and purchase warranty which won't be available if you bring the items from overseas. The benefit of coming with lighter carry will be greater than carrying more weights via Airplane. Of course, if you already have something you really like and if they are not weighing too much, go ahead and bring them over.

Chapter 1 - Reference links

Setting up bank prior to your visit

- *www.commbank.com.au/moving-to-australia/checklist.html*

- *www.commbank.com.au/moving-to-australia/banking.html*

Australian customs guide on which items are allowed to bring

- *www.abf.gov.au/entering-and-leaving-australia/can-you-bring-it-in*

- *www.agriculture.gov.au/biosecurity-trade/travelling/moving-immigrating*

Chapter 2 –
First day

WEATHER AND CLIMATE IN SYDNEY

By each season

Australia has 4 distinctive seasons as below for each corresponding month.

Spring season - September, October, November

This is flower blooming season. Average temperature is around 25 degrees °C. Flower festivals are noticeable attractions during this season. Warnings goes to those who has hay-fevers and allergies.

Summer season - December, January, February

This is the hottest season. Average temperature is around 35 degrees °C.

There is a high chance of bush fire will occur, and Australia Government have implemented various ways to prevent and control otherwise can be uncontrollable and very dangerous. Bush fire can easily spread out wide across the nation. There will be serious penalty for those who triggers any fire (e.g., not fully extinguishing cigarette butt or camp fire) no matter how small it maybe.

Autumn season - March, April, May

This is season just before winter starts, and while the average temperate is close to Spring tempature, the overall humidity level starts to drop significantly compared to Summary season. Average temperature is around 25 degrees °C. In the morning lowest temperature can reach 7-8 degrees °C in the metropolitan areas of Sydney. Watch out for having dry and itchy skin and prevent it by applying plenty of moisturisers.

Winter season - June, July, August

Winter in Sydney is cold; however, temperature does not reach below 0 degree °C.

Snow falls during winter season towards Southern part of NSW state. Jindabyne / Thredbo is about 5-6 hours distance from Sydney by car which is a great place to visit for skiing or just to see lot of snow in the mountain area during the winter season.

Geographically speaking, as you go further away from Sydney, locations towards south or west of the ocean, you will find the temperature during the winter tends to get colder and during the summer it gets hotter than Sydney area.

WHAT TO WEAR ON ARRIVAL

December, January, and February in Sydney

Weather will be warm and even some of the days weather will be hot. Make sure to bring your sunglasses as sun in Australia will expose you under direct UV (unlike most of other areas in the earth).

You may want to factor in your origin of your destination and your natural body temperatures based on your biological factors such as age and sex. If you are coming from the area well below 33 latitude, Sydney (located in 33 latitude) weather during these months may not be too hot for you.

I suggest you consider the following:

Check the degree of latitude by each country here:

- https://www.distancelatlong.com/all/countries/

Also, supposedly if you are aged over 65 and body weight below 60kg you might find Sydney weather during these months chilly and cold for you. The age and weight of body is not the exact measure for guidance, but it is important to apply your natural body temperature compared to others in different age group and body size and don't assume the same.

In either of case, Sydney weather will be just right with similar type of clothes you already have in your existing wardrobe will suffice.

Be prepared that rain will be coming down at any time of the day in the week, of the month in the year. In Australia, raining is part of all year around weather.

Arriving during March, April, May in Sydney

Weather will be pleasant (especially if you find February month hot) during Autumn season. Characteristic of Autumn is that weather starts to become less humid and therefore, you will find evening cold if you are not wearing warm jackets or long sleeve cover.

If you have met any one of the above-described destination of origin and biological factors, you will find these months quite chill.

Arriving during September and October in Sydney

It is official spring season, and you will find lot of flowers will be welcoming you along with pollens (which can be cause of hay fever and allergies). Though it is a beautiful season, be prepared and expect low temperature in the evening, so be sure to carry a cardigan or a jumper.

Arriving during June, July, and Aug in Sydney

This is a winter season. Sydney winter is not like USA or Canada where it can be very cold (reaches minus Celsius degrees in any days during their Winter months Dec, Jan, and Feb). Sydney's June, July and Aug will be, however, cold enough for you unless you have been living in Northern Europe or Canada, so be sure to have enough warm clothes packed before you come. Get a nice jacket, or woollen jumper. Layering your inner materials is highly recommended.

Plus, be prepared that indoor temperature in Sydney tends to be on the lower side due to traditional building / construction materials were chosen purposely to draw the internal heat out rather than to retain it during hot summer naturally, making some of the homes make you feel cold while you are in door. However, not to worry, wearing many layers of clothes is one sure way of keeping yourself away from getting cold. Also, selecting north and east facing window home is a wise chose to retain as much as sun light and warmth naturally throughout the day, which will help you save energy cost of using heater.

MUST DO - ON ARRIVAL

As you arrive to Sydney Airport

Make sure to get mobile sim card and set up your first mobile account and activate at the counter. Do not leave the counter unless you have successfully able to make phone call. Initially try sign up for cheap options - network in Australia is generally stable - and there for if you are ever in doubt sign up with a provider which has internet and phone call included 'SIM only plan or pre-paid' without any locking contract. Once you settle in, phone number can be transferred over easily to another network of your choice.

Time of arrival

Sydney's normal business operating hour is 9am - 5pm, except on Thursdays for extended hours of operation is 9am - 9pm. Of course, there are convenient stores and essential groceries shops such as Woolworths, Coles operates generally till 10pm at any given days, however, be prepared that most of shops will be closed during evening times. If you are arrival time is at late evening, I suggest you go straight to your accommodation and take a good rest. Prepare for essential medicines and basics needs for the night so that you won't have to wonder outside to do shopping.

Decide mode of travel to your accommodation

Research your arrival destination location and best mode of travel from airport using Google map before departure. Google in Australia is very well adopted, and it is reliable source of information to determine your route and travel mode options.

In case you have lot of luggage to carry or arriving late to the airport in Sydney (i.e., approximately 10pm or after), do consider a vehicle option. The cost of travel however is dear. You can easily expect $100 AUD on average (distance of 20km) using taxi service or car share such as Uber, Didi, or Ola. To use this, you will have to install the app prior to arrival to Sydney and create an user login.

Public Train is available from Sydney International Airport. Cost is $21 AUD on average (Mascot airport to Hornsby station). Actual price of the ticket will vary based on the final destination.

Exact fare can be checked on Transport NSW

- https://transportnsw.info

Great thing about this travel option is you can immediately use your credit card to tap on and off. Alternatively, you can purchase Opal ticket at the train ticket counter. When your journey starts to or from the Airport, the fee is higher than usual public transport fee as 'airport' trip cost is added.

Public Bus option is available which won't be costing airport travel fee; however, this is only recommended to use only if you can arrive directly to your accommodation without any transfers without much luggage to carry.

Chapter 2 - Reference links

Degree of latitude by country

https://www.distancelatlong.com/all/countries

Transport NSW

https://transportnsw.info

Chapter 3 -
First month

WHERE TO STAY

Airbnb

Airbnb is recommended if you require a booking to be arranged for rather short term stay of a specific location of your preference. Long term booking may be available, however, your cost of stay will be calculated on daily rate which is higher than average daily rate than other accommodation.

Community website

The community forum website provides information for possible accommodation.

> **TIP:** Search them online or on Facebook group. Also, find them at international grocery stores.

Flatmate

This is an ideal option for single person who is travelling. Flatmate site (https://flatmates.com.au) has listing of a room lease which is listed by either owner of property or a person who is already renting the place to share the property and cost of bills.

Rent

Rent won't be ideal at this stage on your arrival. To rent a place, you will require to provide documents to prove your identity, Salary, and your history of previous rentals or where you have stayed. Also, as you start rental, utility needs to be arranged and pay the bills separately. Rent is recommended to start around 2-3 months after your first arrival.

Hotel/Motel

Hotel or Motel is most suited for 2-3 days stay until you can move to your next accommodation. However, do plan carefully as cost of transport via taxi or uber can be substantial if you are having to take much luggage.

HOW TO MOVE AROUND

Public Transport

Public Transport in Sydney Australia is reliable and well connected to each suburb. Sydney has total 5 modes of public transport: Train, Bus, Metro, Tram, and Ferry. 2 major public transports will be Train and Bus which has widest connecting points throughout Sydney. Ferry is unique to Sydney which travels on the water. Metro and Trams are most recently development in Sydney, connecting in higher frequency designed to cover pockets of in-between locations where public transports either Bus or Train were not previously available.

Visit Transport NSW https://transportnsw.info to see various mode of travel option.

Walk

Walk path in Sydney is extremely well designed alongside vehicle road throughout the suburbs. Enjoy your stroll to nearby shops, parks, or even bush walking in the national parks. If you are lucky to find a work which is located near to your home, you might just be able to walk to your office.

Bicycle / E-Bike

Bicycle or E-bike are great options if you are into exercise and clean energy solutions.

Sydney has road regulations required by vehicle to allow enough space (minimum 1 meter) and give ways to Bicycles on the road, making the riding bicycle safe for a long travel.

Refer to:

- www.nsw.gov.au/driving-boating-and-transport/roads-safety-and-rules/sharing-road-overtaking-and-merging/sharing-roads-bicycles

One thing to note is, anyone who rides bicycle must wear a helmet, otherwise, you can be fined amount over $300 AUD by police.

TIP: Always wear a helmet when riding a bicycle for your safety and to avoid getting a hefty fine!

Refer to:

- www.transport.nsw.gov.au/roadsafety/bicycle-riders/road-rules-for-bicycle-riders

Scooter / Motorcycle

In Australia, Scooter, and Motorcycle registration to the number of cars registered is 1:10. They are handy mode of travel, if you are already familiar with riding it. You will require Class R (Rider) licence to drive either Scooter or Motorcycle. This licence is separate from vehicle licence which is Class C (Car Driver) type licence.

Refer to:

- www.nsw.gov.au/driving-boating-and-transport/driver-and-rider-licences

Car ride

Uber, Didi, Ola or Taxi are commonly available Car ride option. You can make a booking and have payment method ready prior departure. If you are considering making a booking using your overseas bank account or credit card, please do make the booking in advance if the international transaction has been allowed prior to leaving the country.

Car sharing

Uber car share and GoGet are the great option for your car share method. This is slightly different from Car Ride which takes you as a passenger. In Car Sharing mode, you will be the driver upon leasing the car for the set amount of time. You can lease a car as little period as 1 hour.

Car rental

Car Rental is more a traditional method to hire and more widely available with major fleet service providers such as, Hertz, Avis, SIXT, Thrifty, Budget Rent a Car, Europcar etc. You might also be able to take advantage of existing membership benefit (for the internationally networked chain) or discounts which usually comes with selected partnering credit cards or hotel chains.

CAR OWNERSHIP

Owning your very car is a great option to consider especially if you have a family with you and there are many requirements for your settlement to be fulfilled, such as buying and carrying your groceries, getting your furniture, go out for an outdoor sightseeing, getting to and from places and many more reasons. Especially in Sydney, lot of items are cheaper as you buy in bulk quantity or in volume. Considering that in mind, being able to carry a bit more will help you to save money in long run.

Second hand vs Brand New

Deciding which car to buy can be a mind-boggling task. One rule of thumb to be guided by is your available 'budget' and stick to that for purchase of car decision.

Deciding on brand new car is not as tricky as purchasing a second-hand car. The biggest benefit of brand new car is it usually comes with 5 - 7 years manufacture warranty and at the time of purchase, your registration fee is included which can save you money around $700 - $1,000 AUD depends on the market value of your vehicle.

Refer to:

- www.carsguide.com.au for your research and navigate listings of all types of vehicles.
- www.fairtrading.nsw.gov.au/cars-and-other-vehicles/buying-and-selling-a-car/buying-a-used-car

for what are the things to lookout for second hand car purchase.

Second hand car - overall market and decision

In Australia, second hand car market is highly active, and you can obtain transparent data that will help towards making informed decision. For a history of vehicle with the registration number, visit:

www.service.nsw.gov.au/transaction/order-a-vehicle-history-report

Alternatively, you can check the details of car history using 'VIN' number which is uniquely associated number to the manufactured vehicle. This report is not free, however, it is highly recommended. Visit: www.carhistory.com.au

---

TIP: Check car's accident history, any financial liability, ownership of car, and overall condition history of vehicle to determine a fair market value to negotiate purchase price.

Once you are assured with all the details on the paper records of the second-hand car you are interested to purchase, the next step is to arrange a physical vehicle inspection. NRMA and Redbook inspect offers a service starting from $270 AUD for an expert to go out and do a thorough check on the vehicle with comprehensive report afterwards.

Visit:

- www.mynrma.com.au/cars-and-driving/car-servicing/mobile-vehicle-inspections
- www.redbookinspect.com.au/prepurchase

Arranging payment

In terms of payment of car, you can pay with your cash saving. However, it will be difficult to afford highly priced car, especially if you just moved over to Sydney Australia and there will be many other costs to spend.

Alternative option is, getting a financial loan arranged directly from the car dealer selling the car especially for a brand-new car. Car dealers will run promotions with low interest rate to sell the car time to time.

And the last option is, if you have been staying in Australia with a job for over 3-6 months, on the basis you are a permanent resident, you can get a financial loan arranged from bank.

> **IMPORTANT:**
>
> With a Temporary visa, loan may not be approved.

ONGOING COST OF CAR OWNERSHIP

Maintenance cost

Price of second-hand car will range from as low as few $100 AUD to Millions of dollars in AUD. Which is the reflection of availability of wide range of vehicles which varies by many different factors such as quality, make, models, and years of car. Low prices don't necessarily mean a low in quality, rather it would most likely have driven for many mileages (kms) in comparison to the age of the vehicle.

By law, in Australia NSW, you must have your vehicle check for 'road worthiness' once it passes 5 years since the year of manufacture. To do that, you will have to visit a mechanic and ask for 'pink slip' which is known as vehicle registration check - certification. This will usually cost you around $50 - $100 AUD.

> **IMPORTANT:**
>
> Road worthiness check is mandatory for any vehicle over 5 years old. Without it, vehicle registration won't be renewed.

Usually for second hand or any vehicle over 5 years old, it is very common that regular maintenance is required, involving cost of repair or small maintenance fee - which you should budget it for around $1,000 - $2,000 AUD per year.

TIP: Refer to Insuring your car section to understand what other costs are involved.

Apart from the above-mentioned costs, there are three more area of cost which will incur each year. These are 1. Mandatory vehicle registration, 2. Mandatory insurance (CTP) and 3. Optional insurance (third-party) and we will explore each of them in the below.

Registering your car

Mandatory vehicle registration

Mandatory vehicle registration gives your vehicle right to drive on the road by assigning a number plate for your car. The cost will depend on the vehicle model and most of private vehicle (e.g., sedan) will cost around $400 AUD for 12 months, requiring renewal before expiry each year. Check the cost of registration for your vehicle on this page: https://myrta.com/myRego/pages/content/rc/RegistrationCalculator.page

There is an option choose your own registration number at additional annual fee via 'Service NSW'.
Refer to: www.myplates.com.au

Note, each state has separately governed and managed vehicle registration differently from NSW state.

For a brand-new car, registration will be coming with it and cost is usually covered by the manufacturer's dealer.

Transferring registration after purchasing second-hand car

For a second-hand car, the registration needs to be transferred (ownership transfer) from original owner to yourself and you will get to take on remaining valid period of registration. To do that go to:

www.service.nsw.gov.au/transaction/transfer-a-vehicle-registration

---

TIP: make sure you transfer the Rego into your name within 14 days of acquiring the vehicle. If you wait longer than 14 days, you'll have to pay a late transfer fee as well as the registration stamp duty.

Insuring your car

Mandatory accidental human injury insurance - CTP

Compulsory Third Party (CTP) Insurance – aka Green Slip - is mandatory insurance covering human injury aspect.

CTP will cover accident compensation paid to people physically or psychologically injured in a car accident. A common misconception is that CTP covers damage to cars and property when, in fact, it doesn't.
Refer to www.greenslips.nsw.gov.au

Provider of this insurances are AAMI, Allianz, GIO, NRMA, QBE and Youi as of 2023. **The CPT insurers list can be found from here:** www.sira.nsw.gov.au/insurance-coverage/CTP-insurance-Green-Slips/buying-a-green-slip/contact-an-insurer

Optional third-party insurance

Third party insurance is not mandatory and optional to the car owner's discretion. It is, however, highly recommended to take a 'comprehensive third-party car insurance' as it will cover all aspects of cost that will incur for your car damage and other person's car damage with an access fee.

There are many providers of third-party insurance to choose from. For the above providers, you can do a google search or **compare them on the below websites to find the best offer at the lowest cost.**

- www.finder.com.au/car-insurance-nsw
- www.comparethemarket.com.au/car-insurance/australia/new-south-wales/
- www.iselect.com.au/car-insurance/

E-toll

For faster highway access, toll is collected in NSW. To use toll road, you can get e-toll tag for your car. This is not mandatory, however, it is lot more convenient if you get e-toll tag for your car, so that as you are driving in Sydney you won't have to pay the fee after passing the toll road.

Additional manual processing fee will be added to the toll usage fee if you don't already have an account.

Refer to: www.myetoll.transport.nsw.gov.au

Alternatively, on Google map, unselect 'toll road' option on direction search setting to make sure to avoid Toll Road when you are driving.

Road Rules

Parking and road rule violation has consequence with a strict fine and sometime with demerit points. It is impossible to ignore or influence it with bribe or position of power.

Fine amount and demerit point varies on each type offences and it can range as low as $100 to and maximum fine and penalty up to $ 17,740 AUD as of 2023. The fine rate is always subject to change.

Maximum limit of your demerit point (allowance) is depending on the type of licence you have. When you reach the maximum, you will lose your driving licence. Note, during public holiday timing demerit point will double.

Refer to demerits and penalty guide here:
www.nsw.gov.au/driving-boating-and-transport/demerits-penalties-and-offences

WHERE TO BUY FOOD

In Sydney there are major grocers easy to find from most of people's home. Try to locate nearby Coles or Woolworths, Aldi, or IGA on Google map for decision of your home location.

Apart from above mentioned grocers, you will be able to see vegetable grocers along with broad ethnic based grocers such as Asian, and specific nationality-based grocers. The most available ones are Indian, Korean, Chinese, Japanese followed by Philippines, Middle Eastern, Greek, Italian, German, French grocers.

> **TIP:** Shopping night in Sydney is on every 'Thursday'. This is a great time of the week to catch up with shopping and groceries especially if you are planning on something for the weekend.

MANAGING BANKING

Create a bank account

If you have not yet already set up your bank account prior to your arrival, that is fine. You have more choices to choose from when you arrive.

Big 4 banks

In Australia and Sydney, you will find below banks most commonly available. These are 4 major banks in Australia you can choose from to setup your account.

- CommBank
- ANZ
- NAB
- Westpac

> **TIP:** Each bank will have a slightly a different process of signing you up initially. Either apply the account via online or apply directly by visiting the branch with your passport and visa details.

Other reputable and trustworthy banks are available such as, St George, Citibank, HSBC, Bank of China, Bankwest, Macquarie Bank, Bendigo and Adelaide Bank etc.

MOBILE PHONE, INTERNET

Connect to internet and phone

Mobile phone

It is highly recommended to get your first mobile phone from the first day of arrival regardless of provider of service.

Major network providers are Telstra, Optus and Vodafone, and there are more available with unique coverage area with deals provided by TPG, Lebara, Lycamobile Coles, ALDI mobile, Kogan, Belong, iiNet, Dodo and many more.

IMPORTANT:

It is a good idea to check their service coverage of your home location and your work area as each service providers have certain location without coverage.

Broadband

Internet in Australia is available as 5G wireless network and NBN wired network - national broadband network (fibre optics connection). Not all areas have access to full high speed though. Unless you are avid gamer requiring high speed internet non-stop, Australia's internet connection is reasonably fast for majority' people use for home and work purposes.

In addition to the above providers for broadband network, you can compare price and service availability from other providers as well.

Compare broadband network:
www.whistleout.com.au/Broadband/Guides/australia-internet-providers

---

TIP: It is possible to switch your plan upon lack of coverage thanks for strong consumer law protection exist in Australia, however, to avoid any hassle it is good idea to check the coverage from their website.

Chapter 3 – Reference links

Public Transport - NSW

- *https://transportnsw.info*

Rules for Bicycle riding

- *www.nsw.gov.au/driving-boating-and-transport/roads-safety-and-rules/sharing-road-overtaking-and-merging/sharing-roads-bicycles*

- *www.transport.nsw.gov.au/roadsafety/bicycle-riders/road-rules-for-bicycle-riders*

Rules for Scooter / Motorcycle

- *www.nsw.gov.au/driving-boating-and-transport/driver-and-rider-licences*

Purchasing your car

- *www.carsguide.com.au*

- *www.fairtrading.nsw.gov.au/cars-and-other-vehicles/buying-and-selling-a-car/buying-a-used-car*

Second hand car

- *www.service.nsw.gov.au/transaction/order-a-vehicle-history-report*

- *www.carhistory.com.au*

- *www.mynrma.com.au/cars-and-driving/car-servicing/mobile-vehicle-inspections*

- *www.redbookinspect.com.au/prepurchase*

Vehicle registration

- *https://myrta.com/myRego/pages/content/rc/RegistrationCalculator.page*

- *www.myplates.com.au*

Vehicle registration transfer

- *www.service.nsw.gov.au/transaction/transfer-a-vehicle-registration*

CTP (Greenslips) insurance

- *www.greenslips.nsw.gov.au*

- *www.sira.nsw.gov.au/insurance-coverage/CTP-insurance-Green-Slips/buying-a-green-slip/contact-an-insurer*

Third Party insurance

- *www.finder.com.au/car-insurance-nsw*

- *www.comparethemarket.com.au/car-insurance/australia/new-south-wales/*

- *www.iselect.com.au/car-insurance/*

E-Toll

- *https://www.myetoll.transport.nsw.gov.au*

Road Rules

- *www.nsw.gov.au/driving-boating-and-transport/demerits-penalties-and-offences*

Broadband

- *www.whistleout.com.au/Broadband/Guides/australia-internet-providers*

Chapter 4 -
First year

IMPORTANT FORM OF ID

100 points of ID

In Australia, important form of ID documents are Australian Driver licence and Passport. There are no central government-controlled identity cards, which makes Drivers licence most reliable identification document followed by Passport.

In most of cases, you will require 100 points of ID, for instance to apply for a mobile phone plan or to apply for rental property, you will require to provide 100 points of ID.

100 points of ID comprises of various types of information to verify your identity. The system requires that an individual provide a mix of documents, as either originals or certified copies to establish that an individual is who they claim to be.

There are two types of ID which are primary and secondary. **Refer to this guide for what makes the points of each ID:** https://www.afp.gov.au/sites/default/files/PDF/NPC-100PointChecklist-18042019.pdf

This is a very useful guide to refer to - **how 100 points can be made in different combinations when you just arrived in Sydney**: www.sydneymovingguide.com/100-points-id/

Photo Card/ID

The most useful and widely accepted form of ID locally in NSW is Driver licence (apart from Passport is designed more for international travel and ID proof for that matter). If you don't know how to drive already, photo ID is your best alternative for your ID instead. Carrying passport all the time is not so practical. **Apply it from Service NSW website:** www.service.nsw.gov.au/transaction/apply-for-a-nsw-photo-card.

Student ID

If you are a Student, Student ID will be issued. This is not as powerful to replace your driver's licence as an authoritative document, however, this is important if you want to take all the possible benefits available during your stay in Australia Sydney as a student. You will likely be able to get 'student discount' by presenting the card in participating retail or online stores.

IMPORTANT:

Please note, in Sydney NSW there is no student discount fare available for public transport if you are an 'international student'. However, the student fare discount is available in Melbourne VIC for international students.

Driver licence

In case you have an overseas driver's licence, you can transfer your licence through Service NSW. To do so, you might have to take a driving test to transfer your driver licence as a full driver's licence, depending on the country of original licence. What this means is that existing licence let you skip the requirement of L, red P and green P which otherwise will be required to be taken prior to obtaining a full licence.

TIP: Driver licence issued from certain countries and jurisdictions are exempted from driving test to transfer it to Australian Driver licence.

Make sure to check list of countries of test exemptions: www.nsw.gov.au/driving-boating-and-transport/driver-and-rider-licences/visiting-or-moving-to-nsw/moving-your-overseas-licence/knowledge-and-driving-test-exemptions

---

Driving with overseas driver licence and Road Rules

You are allowed to drive with your overseas driver licence lawfully by following the road rules for 3 months for Permanent Resident visa holder or 6 months for Temporary visa holder.

Please refer to corresponding road rule guides

For car: www.nsw.gov.au/driving-boating-and-transport/driver-and-rider-licences/licence-publications
For motorcycle: www.nsw.gov.au/sites/default/files/2021-05/motorcycle-riders-handbook.pdf

Transferring an overseas driver licence

Temporary VISA holder has 6 months before to transfer the licence to NSW driver licence.

Permanent VISA holder has 3 months before to transfer the licence to NSW driver licence.

> **IMPORTANT:**
>
> From 1 July 2023, penalties will apply to a temporary visa holder who has resided in NSW for a continuous period of six months or more, and who continues to drive in NSW on their overseas licence. They will be driving a vehicle unlicenced.
>
> It is proposed that a fine of $603 will apply for a first offence and a fine of $924 will apply for a second or subsequent offence. A maximum penalty of $2200 (20 penalty units) may be imposed by a court.

Refer to transferring an overseas driver licence guide: www.nsw.gov.au/driving-boating-and-transport/driver-and-rider-licences/visiting-or-moving-to-nsw

Driving test – Learner licence

If you don't have the driver's licence already, you need to try for driving licence from learner's driver licence first, and gradually obtain P1 and P2 licence to gain full licence.

TIP: When you are over age of 25, there is no requirement to fill in learners drive logbook.

Driving test – Full licence

What is important note is that Driving rules are strictly followed in Australia. Therefore, driving exam is equally strict. Not only you have to demonstrate that you can manoeuvre the vehicle, but more than a skill, you need to be able to demonstrate you are driving accordingly to road safety regulation.

If you didn't pass more than 90% out of 100% required passing criteria, you will fail the driving test. I strongly suggest you seek out driving trainer before your test.

Refer to driving test guide

www.nsw.gov.au/sites/default/files/2021-08/guide-to-driving-test.pdf

Also, you will require a roadworthy vehicle to that you can use it during the test. Unless you have a car and a person who can help you take to the exam location and bring you back in case you fail the test, make sure to borrow training instructor's vehicle and arrange the booking of their hours as part of the test arrangement.

Refer to test fees: www.nsw.gov.au/driving-boating-and-transport/driver-and-rider-licences/fees

FINDING RENTAL ACCOMODATION

Renting

Rental is a good way to start your long stay residence after your initial couple of months stay in Australia. **Start look for rental properties in** www.domain.com.au or www.realestate.com.au

Following are the suggested steps for rental property search.

Fix your Budget

Firstly, set a budget for weekly spend. This is important part of the process. Upon deciding how much you are feeling comfortable to spend and you want to make sure to find a property that meets that budget criteria.

> **TIP:** ideal amount of rental is recommended to be no more than 1/3 of your earning

Search can be flexible to accommodate slight increase, however, try to stick to your budget.

Location

Secondly, decide on a suburb you wish to live. This might be a challenging decision as you are not fully aware of all the areas and options. Best starting point is to look for a suburb which is most accessible to where you need to spend majority of your time. Then look for a place which is closer to access major groceries.

> **TIP:** If you need to be at work most of the time, try to find home that you can easily travel back and from within an hour of door-to-door travel (including walking, waiting for the transport to arrive) by taking public transport.

Inspection

Thirdly, upon selecting nominated homes that are in your desired suburb, check 'open home' visiting hours & inspection days. This open home session will be usually hosted by the 'real estate agent' who will be representing the homeowner on behalf.

If you are interested to apply, you can take a form which is to be given by the real-estate agent and submit it either on the spot or via online with details of your job, income, and referee.

IMPORTANT:

One thing to note is that Australia being traditionally a warm continent, most of homes have been built to be 'cool' rather than 'warm' naturally. So, when inspecting home, follow the 'inspection points not to miss' section.

Inspection points not to miss

1. **Direction of the sun:** best side is North and East facing and followed by North facing. This direction will ensure you can get bright sun coming through entire day during all season and during summer the direction of sun is angled making less heat will be generated towards indoor. If you decide to select low level floor facing south - winter time you will find the place being too cold, requiring heating 24/7.

2. **Hot water generation:** all the water in Australian units or home is always centrally heated. It means there is no requirement for any individual geyser. However, do make sure to ask to try test the hot water by switching on the tab to be able to tell how quickly hot water comes out. Ideally it should not take more than 4-5 seconds to get a very nice hot water. If hot water is taking time to come out or not too hot, it is most likely that the hot water tank generator is old requiring a replacement.

Putting down the Deposit

Fourthly, only if you want to continue with the rental property you will only then have to make a non-refundable deposit of 1 week (this will however be added towards total rental bond later on upon the selection) worth of rent along with application document which contains your details, work, income and referees to certify your income. If you don't have a work yet but have enough finance to arrange the rent, it is possible to the put the application. However, there is a possibility of rejection when there are many more other candidates out there who can provide greater guarantee of payment.

If you get selected, Rental agreement take place. There will be 4 weeks of bond which is refundable that you will have to pay in addition to the deposit.

IMPORTANT:

Make sure that the property condition you are renting be the same as when you started the rent when you leave the place (finishing the rent).

What you need to do once secured rent

1. Take all the pictures to the close-up detail and keep your own evidence to prove the condition when you initially entered the property. These pictures will come handy later when you need to provide evidences.

2. If there are any issue that you spot - such as faulty or damaged - such as kitchen range hood light, door, hole in the window screen (mosquito net), scratched paint on the walls, you should inform the property owner (or the real-estate agent). Do make sure to report it back to the agency or the owner within 7 days of your initial residency and ask for it to be fixed.

   Likewise regular maintenance onus is on you to ensure the property is well taken care by giving clear communication whenever any requirement to fix arises. Cost to fix will have to be covered by the owner of the property unless damage was caused due to your own mishandling during your stay later.

BOND

At the beginning of the tenancy, a landlord or agent can only ask a tenant to pay a bond (maximum four weeks rent) up to two weeks rent in advance. For example, $440 AUD per week rent, bond is calculated as: $440 X 4 = $1,760 AUD

For the protection of tenant, the rental bond gets stored separately from the owner and the agent. The bond gets stored to a trust (arranged by the agent under government mandate) which can be returned upon your exit of property after the agreed period of rent.

Only case you might fail to get the full or entire return of bond is when you have damaged or deteriorated the condition of the property. If you think your assessment of rental condition is unfairly done by the real-estate agent, you can challenge to the ombudsmen for fair assessment and outcome that you seek (i.e., full refund of bond).

Ongoing monthly payment

The monthly figure is calculated on the daily rate as there is not 4 weeks in every month - e.g., Weekly rent divided by 7, times 365, divided by 12.

The calculations for a property for $440 AUD per week rent would be:

$440 / 7 = $62.86

$62.86 X 365 = $22,942.86

$22,942.86 / 12 = $1,911.90

For $440 AUD per week rent, $1,911.90 AUD needs to be paid every agreed date on the month.

Cleaning at the end of rent

Make sure to clean the property upon exit (end of term).

Expected cost is $400 AUD for about 2 bed and 1 bathroom to clean the entire home and $200 - $400 AUD for steam carpet floor cleaning. Benefit is that not only they will give a very thorough cleaning, and if any issues raise, the real-estate can raise the concern directly with the cleaners.

How does Rental works and what are the obligations:

- *www.nsw.gov.au/housing-and-construction/renting-a-place-to-live/renting-a-property-nsw/starting-a-lease/paying-a-rental-bond*

- *www.fairtrading.nsw.gov.au/housing-and-property/renting/rental-bonds-online*

- *www.fairtrading.nsw.gov.au/housing-and-property/renting/starting-a-tenancy*

MORTGAGE PROPERTY

Buying your first home

In Australia, the most common instrument used to obtain a property asset (which will be your first home) is via Mortgage loan.

Enquire and consult on mortgage loan

Firstly, you are eligible to arrange a mortgage loan if you are PR holder. Reach out to the banks directly to arrange the best deal.

IMPORTANT:

If you do not hold Permanent Residency Visa but hold temporary residence visa, you will have to pay additional fee under the guide of Foreign Investment Review Board (FIRB) body and property law. Breach of this guide result in penalty.

It is still possible to arrange a mortgage without having PR visa, however, it can be tricky process for first home buyer. In such case, it is best to engage mortgage broker instead.

Prepare for minimum required deposit amount

You will require a deposit amount. It must be available for at least minimum 5% but best is to have 20% or more of the purchase price of the property as a deposit amount. If your loan deposit is less than 20%, you will have to pay LMI (lenders mortgage insurance) to protect bank's risk of possibility of your loan getting defaulted. LMI can be however financed within the mortgage loan together.

Calculate your LMI:

www.loancalculatoraustralia.com.au/lenders-mortgage-insurance-calculator

Stamp Duty (Transfer Duty)

Stamp duty is a mandatory fee for everyone. In NSW, Stamp duty is exempted for the first home buyers purchasing up to $800,000 AUD, then there is concessional rate of duty for homes up to $1,000,000 AUD. This is to encourage increased ownership of a property for everyone in NSW. Find a property and take advantage of this duty exemption.

Calculate Stamp Duty:

www.apps09.revenue.nsw.gov.au/erevenue/calculators/fhba.php

Temporary Residence's surcharge

If you are a temporary resident, check your eligibility to purchase a property without having to pay 8% surcharge purchaser duty as an additional fee.

Check your estimated charges:
www.revenue.nsw.gov.au/taxes-duties-levies-royalties/transfer-duty/surcharge-purchaser-duty/surcharge-for-individuals.

Foreign Investment Review Board - FIRB

IMPORTANT:

Penalty will be imposed if you purchase a property as a temporary resident without an approval from FIRB.

Refer to FIRB's guide and definition on temporary residence regarding purchasing a residence property:
https://firb.gov.au/sites/firb.gov.au/files/guidance-notes/02_GN_FIRB.pdf

Prepare for other additional charges

All add up, you might find purchase price (monthly payout) is not necessarily cheaper than the rent. In fact, the cost of home ownership is much greater than renting it especially in NSW. This is due to high demand of purchase and home ownership desire exist in Sydney region.

Owning a property, however, comes with great sense of achievement and joy that a permanent settlement can offer. Make sure to check of all the cost involved in the process of purchasing a home for your decision.

For more information on possible fees associated with mortgage please refer to: www.mortgagechoice.com.au.

Refinancing your mortgage

Interest rate

In Australia, unlike US, interest rate can't be locked in for a long period, requiring frequent (every 1 - 3 years) refinancing. You can get longer period financing however, very unlikely be better off by that arrangement based on how mortgage products are developed for Australia. Therefore, refinancing for a better home loan rate can be helpful.

Valuation

Valuation of property is the most important aspect for the next round of refinancing. What this means is you will have more negotiation power to get better interest rate and products.

> **IMPORTANT:**
>
> Valuation of property is the most important aspect for the next round of refinancing.

Valuation is arranged by the bank, through independent assessors during your refinancing consultation.

Valuation estimation assumes that 'every single' property in that location is out for sales all at the same time. Of course, that is unlikely scenario, but this is a useful to note.

What will determine the valuation is bank's risk appetite to the market and interest rate (cash rate bank set by Reserve Bank of Australia) at the time of the valuation (the greater the interest rate, the lower the valuation of the housing). Valuation will fluctuate and will vary by each bank, and it is not identical to 'transaction/market price'.

Market Price

Your 'selling or buying price' which is known as a 'market price' does not 100% reflection of your home 'valuation'.

It can be risky if your home valuation drops significantly compared to your equity (what you actually paid off compared to valuation of the property), which might result you to pay the difference of the drop back to bank. In that case, you might have to forcefully sell the property which you have purchased.

TIP: It is not recommended to purchase any property that has the same or lower valuation than what is offered sell price.

Equity

IMPORTANT:

You will have to pay LMI again if your equity is 20% or greater when you want to refinance with another bank.

Equity is calculated based on (Bank's valuation of the property 'minus' what you still owe to bank). If the Equity is less than 20% of the outstanding bank loan, LMI is again required to be paid when refinancing. Some banks don't accept refinancing if you don't own 20% of Equity.

TYPES OF ACCOMMODATION

There are many different types of accommodation you can consider as below; take a note on how each are different.

Strata & Council fee involved properties

Unit / Apartment

Unit (without lift) is generally an old style of building, built mostly with bricks and it tends to have no lifts but only uses stairs. It is structurally very sturdy and strong.

Whereas, Apartment usually has a lift and considered to be high rise with more than 6 levels.

There is quarterly Strata (building management) fee. Usually it is charged around $1,000 - $2,000 AUD per quarter to be paid after your purchase of unit.

> **TIP:** Strata fee is indirectly indicating condition of the property. Such as structural issue or any maintenance requirement (building quality) can be foretold if the strata has continuously been going up year on year.

Usually more the facility there is (e.g., swimming pool and lift and security guard) the strata free is greater. The cost is divided by total number of the property and proportionally to the square meter size of the unit.

In addition to Strata fee, Council fee needs to be paid for yearly and figure will vary depending on the council you belong. On average $1,200 - $1,500 AUD per year needs to be paid for road, streetlights, rubbish dump management, and many other shared facility managements for the area governed under council.

Apartment - Off the plan

Apartment - Off the plan refer to anything that is not yet built but on the premise of it will be built later. You will have to pay the deposit as a down payment and sign the purchase contract and trading early payment with slightly reduced purchase price than what will potentially be appreciated value in the future.

As an investment property it is worth considering its financial benefit. However, this style of property is not recommended for first home purchase requirement due to risky nature of delayed development and changes in structural quality throughout the development.

Strata fee and council fee will be paid upon commencing your full payment to start residence.

Town house

Town house is a great option if you are looking for a house like features (backyards) at a lower price. Town house will present shared community environment as well as the style of home that is consistent with the rest of the home which will require you to help maintain that consistent look and feel.

IMPORTANT:

Property build (structural) quality is very important. Opal and Mascot tower are good infamous example where building was built with high risk and every individual had to evacuate the building. To this date, building is not safe to reside, remaining empty. I strongly encourage you to look up what happened earlier to educate yourself. To avoid any risk, it is recommended to choose an Apartment building which has been built for over 7 ~ 10 years. The builder's insurance gets expired after 7 ~ 10 years and if the strata fee has not gone up substantially after this period, then you can deem that the building has reasonably a good structural quality.

There are strict rules apply in any modification of external wall, or curtain style which in a way behaves very similar to how any unit / Apartment.

Strata fee needs to be paid and it is usually less than Unit / Apartment's amount. Council fee applies the same as Unit / Apartment.

Council Fee only - properties

House with land package

This option give more flexibility of development as you will get to choose bigger land, however, more in the remote area where less residential property already exists. This might be a good option if you want a newly built home, with a large space and willing to wait for couple of years for it to be built. Associated structural quality risk is less than off then plan Apartment building. After moving in, you will have to pay council fee accordingly to the charge rate of the council your home suburb belongs to.

House / House with Granny Flat

House is the best form of property you can have if you want all the flexibility you want with a large space. Sometimes house comes with Granny Flat which has already been built which is allowed up to 1 per one's house backyard space as a detached small home. If you are considering bringing your parents over later, this is a great option.

Recommended place to live

Each area has its own merit and benefits to offer.

Always consider your access to your required facilities, such as school, work, shops and most importantly access to public transport network as listed in the order of highest frequency of travel:

- Metro line
- Train line
- Bus line
- Tram line
- T-way lanes
- Ferry line

TIP: Think about how much travelling time you are willing to spend each day versus mode of travel cost.

Sydney has great public transport network. Each year, state government invests in development of wider connected public transport network to reach further areas. It is a good idea to take full advantage of that.

UTILITY

Unless you are leasing a room (e.g., Airbnb or share accommodation) you will have to arrange your own connection to the following to be ready at the time of moving.

Below is the listing of expected cost for each utility bill for every 3 months.

Water bill

If you are residing within Sydney in NSW, water bill is issued by 'Sydney Water'. Otherwise, water bill will be issued by accordingly to the location where you live in regional areas. On average the cost will be around $200 per every 3 months (each quarter), however it will vary depends on the actual usage amount per household.

> TIP: When you rent, water bill is usually covered by the owner of the property. Check it with real estate agent.

Electricity

Electricity usually is the costliest utility of all. For all the connections, including heating and cooking will require electricity, as many of homes in Australia has electricity stove top. It is very important to find a low-cost electricity provider at the time of sign up.

Compare Electricity and Gas plans:

www.energymadeeasy.gov.au

Average Electricity bill for every 3 months is around $450 - $550 AUD, however, the figure will vary substantially depends on your usage of aircons, or heating and the number of people in the household.

Gas

Gas is not required unless your home is designed with Gas cook top and heats up water using Gas.

Estimated cost is around $200 AUD for every 3 months. You can get a Gas package deal with the same Electricity provider to bring down the cost. Refer to above link to compare the plans from different providers.

MOVING HOME

Cost of moving home

Cost of moving can be high if you don't plan it in advance.

In Australia moving home charge is done by the hour and each hourly fee will cost at least $100 due to high labour service fee charged in general.

Of course, if you have much furniture and if extreme care is required for every single furniture, you will want to move as carefully as possible (i.e., if you have a grand piano, you would certainly don't want it to be damaged).

However, if you have just moved to Australia and chances are you may not have already too many things.

> TIP: As much as you can, pack everything ready to go, with great amount of care using wrappers and protections so that things won't get damaged.

To arrange a service that will provide packing and moving together it will be lot more expensive than simply moving. Budget it around $500 - $2,000 AUD depends on the service you decide to take and the distance you are moving.

If you have friends to help with lift few items, do borrow their hands as it will save few hours in total.

TIP: Get the empty boxes from local grocery stores for free. You may not get the exact size you require, but it won't hurt to ask whether they have any empty carton boxes to throw away.

Kennards self-storage (www.kss.com.au) offers good box buy back options. You can save money this way. Also, they sell second hand first time used box at a much-discounted rate.

ESSENTIAL ITEMS - GROCERY, ELECTRONICS AND FURNITURES

Brand new purchase

Below is the list of places will come helpful for your initial set up for your settlement.

For Essential household items including small furniture

- Kmart
- Big W
- Target
- Bunnings (lot of DIY items will be available if you love being crafty as well)

For White/Electronic goods (such as Fridge and TV)

- Bing Lee
- Harvey Norman
- JB Hi Fi

For Major furniture stores

- IKEA
- Auburn / Alexandria Mega Home Centre (it is worth visiting to see different options and styles at different price range).

Second-hand market

Gumtree & Facebook Market place

In Australia, second hand goods are widely accepted and traded for free. Gumtree (www.gumtree.com.au) and Facebook Marketplace (www.facebook.com/marketplace/) is highly active and most widely covered websites where you will find 'free' furniture which people want to give away.

Not only these are well taken cared by earlier owner, also if you are environmentally conscious person, you are helping for it to not be trashed and recycled.

TIP: You can also 'Upcycle' by giving a new polished look after getting the necessary materials from Bunnings.

By help collecting and using the second hand good, you are literally helping the previous owner of the furniture by saving the requirement of having to make the arrangement for the furniture to be picked up by the council, which not only costs money but hassle of having to move down the furniture.

Charity shops

Throughout Australia, you will find below charity shops, and it is a great place to just drop in to see what is there.

- Vinnies - St
- Salvation Army
- Red Cross
- Lifeline
- Op-shops

The Charity shops sells donated second hand goods and all the earning are used towards helping the community in need.

You will feel not only great by helping those who are in need but also, will have great time visiting fully volunteer operated shop which is beautiful and fun to look around.

HEALTH AND WELLBEING

Where to exercise

In Sydney, you will find many public parks where you can do stretching, or even play team sports such as Rugby, Soccer, Cricket. Search around for swimming pool, Tennis court and other fields where you can enjoy your favourite sports. Gyms are widely available in Sydney in every of suburbs.

Park and recreation

NSW Australia has many public parks around. Look around for those in your suburbs. Check out National Parks in NSW here: www.nationalparks.nsw.gov.au

To save money for car parking in National Park, consider annual pass for entering the national park. www.nationalparks.nsw.gov.au/passes-and-fees

Cycling

You can enjoy your bicycle riding as part of your commute, travel to and from places and as an exercise on the road.

In Sydney, car drivers must give way to the bicycle riders.

There are few important rules to follow to coexist the road where cars or trucks will also be driving together, refer to section under **Chapter 3 – How to move around.**

Where to get medical treatment

If you are not feeling well or to have any check-up, you need to first visit General Practitioner (GP) prior to visiting any specialist or hospitals.

> **IMPORTANT:**
>
> By medical regulations and health system placed in Australia, everyone will have to go through GP first in most of situations.

GP can give guidance on whether you will require to seek further assessment from medical experts who is specialised in a certain field or not.

GP will take necessary level examination and provide health guide, or prescription for medicine you may require.

Benefit to this is an individual don't have to waste time guessing the cause of your symptom.

> **IMPORTANT:**
>
> GP's referral usually covers the cost of any fee that any individual is legally entitled for medical checks or examinations. Without the referral, you may be rejected for check up by the specialist. Also, you won't get full benefit of medical coverage which is provisioned by the state and federal government.

Only exception is, in case of medical emergency, you can visit directly to the emergency in hospital.

TIP: Call 000 for emergency.

Ambulance

Ambulance will cost over $428 AUD each time when it gets called.

> **IMPORTANT:**
>
> If you sign up with Private Health Insurance, the cost is covered as part of Australian health care insurance.

Good news is that most of Australia's visitor visa (excluding short term - travel visa for holiday or for business) requires you to sign up with health insurance during your stay, and it will be covering the Ambulance cost.

For fees and charges of Ambulance:

www.ambulance.nsw.gov.au/our-services/accounts-and-fees/ambulance-coverage-if-you-are-a-nsw-resident

HEALTHCARE SYSTEM

Australian Health Care system

Australian health care system is known to be one of the best in the world, focuses a lot on preventative care to minimise the burden on the Australia's health care infrastructure and for overall wellbeing of every individual and the society.

Let's see how the system is designed and what it means for you.

Medicare

Australia has 'Medicare' system for Australian Citizen and Permanent residents. Medicare is publicly funded universal health care insurance scheme in Australia, operated by the nation's social security department, Services Australia.

What Medicare will cover is fundamental to your health requirement, including and not limited to: GP - general practitioner - visit, blood test, eyesight test, subsidies medicines, public hospital stay and treatment and operations.

Medicare doesn't cover certain part of health-related treatment.

> **IMPORTANT:**
>
> Medicare won't cover the cost of vision enhancing prescription glasses, dentist visit, dental treatment, cosmetic surgery, and other areas which are not considered to be critically life affecting matters.

TIP: Even if you hold Medicare, still I suggest you sign up for Private Health insurance, if you are working and earning an income.

Private Health Insurance

If you are coming to Australia as a permanent resident, you have an option to join any of private health insurance to get 'extras' benefits, covering dental and optical cover and other additional covers such as physiotherapy.

In addition to the above 'extras', the private health insurance comes with an option for 'hospital' cover. This is directly linked to **Lifetime Health Cover loading (LHC):** www.privatehealth.gov.au/health_insurance/surcharges_inc entives/lifetime_health_cover.htm

> **IMPORTANT:**
>
> Private Hospital Cover is an optional insurance which is not mandated, however, if you do not take Private Hospital Cover by 31st birthday, you will be forced to pay a 2% loading for every year you are aged over 30 if you decided to take the insurance later.

If you are 31 years of age or more, and you are Permanent resident migrant, the moment you arrive to Australia as a permanent resident, you have 365 days to sign up for Private Hospital cover before loading starts to apply.

If you're under 31 years of age when you become a permanent resident, you'll have until the 30th of June following your 31st birthday to take out private hospital cover to avoid incurring LHC loading.

> **TIP:** If you are arriving in Australia as a migrant after age of 31, you must receive LHC certificate from Medicare to avoid LHC % getting counted during your first 1 year of arrival.

Medical Levy

Medical Levy (tax payment) is designed by the Australian Government to incentivise voluntarily sign up for a private health insurance.

> **IMPORTANT:**
>
> If you are actively earning an income in Australia, you are subject to pay taxes. What this means is accordingly to your salary you will be paying certain % of your earnings towards 'medical levy' as part of income tax. However, if you sign up for a private health insurance with Hospital cover, you will be exempted from paying 'medical levy'.

Refer to www.ato.gov.au/Individuals/Medicare-and-private-health-insurance/Medicare-levy-surcharge/Medicare-levy-surcharge-income,-thresholds-and-rates/

TIP: You are exempted from healthcare levy surcharge if you earn $93,000 or less.

List of Health Insurers

Main Health Insurance providers are:

- Medibank Private Limited
- Bupa Hi Pty Ltd
- HCF
- nib

Refer to full list of Health care insurers:
www.privatehealth.gov.au/dynamic/insurer

Taking Health Insurance

Get a private hospital health cover if you meet any of the following criteria as a permanent resident:

- You are an income earner and already over age 31;
- You are earning more than $93,001 AUD in Australia (before income tax amount) even if your age is below 31;
- Your family (migrated with your partner) is earning more than $186,001 AUD in Australia (before income tax amount), even you are not earning.

TIP: Get a private extra health cover even if you are not meeting any of the above criteria. Because Private extra cover will come with Ambulance cover, and other health benefits you don't want to miss out on (dental and optics).

Healthcare system - Elderly

If you are not a permanent resident, there won't be Medicare coverage. In this case - you need to opt for specialised health care such as HCF (www.hcf.com.au).

If you, or your parents are aged over 67 and not earning income, and a permanent resident, your Medicare will cover your medical requirements.

Worker's compensation

Any work-related injury is covered by Worker's compensation Australia.

Refer to www.safeworkaustralia.gov.au/workers-compensation

TAX

Tax period

Australia's tax period (also known as financial year) is from July 1st the year prior to the June 30th the year when you lodge the tax.

Lodging tax

Once you have been living in Australia for over 6 months, you are 'resident for taxation purpose'. What does this mean? Unlike those who are visiting Australia purely for holiday or short-term business trip, you will be subject to local resident tax rate as anyone else who has been living in Australia (including Citizens) for many years.

> **IMPORTANT:**
>
> If you are not considered as non-resident for tax purposes, you will have to pay much greater amount of tax than the residents for tax purposes.

Always lodge the tax in Australia. Australia is highly digitised economy which high level of transparency of individual's financial transaction. Avoiding of tax is a crime. You can be criminally convicted for not lodging.

To lodge your tax for the first time, you will need to register in ATO website.

If you have more diversified income or expense to claim, it is also a good idea to lodge through licenced Tax Accountant Agent.

You can either find them nearby shopping mall during tax return period (July - August) or search them online to look for nearby branch office The cost of the accountant fee is usually around $100 - $200 AUD, which can be deducted in the following year tax claim as an 'expense'.

TIP: lodge your tax by the 31 October each year. For most individuals' income situation, ATO has designed a system that is easy for any individual to lodge the tax.

GOOD TO KNOW

Holiday

NSW follows Federal holidays and State holidays.

If you are working professional, try to book holiday time off around that time and enjoy NSW nature.

Also be aware some of the days in NSW do not operate for business so be prepared for that - that is usually Easter day, and Christmas day.

Daylight Savings

NSW follows Eastern Australia Time, and time changes twice within a year, backward and forward.

Daylight Saving Time begins at 2am on the first Sunday in October, when clocks are put forward one hour. It ends at 2am (which is 3am Daylight Saving Time) on the first Sunday in April, when clocks are put back one hour.
Calculate the time differences here:
www.timeanddate.com/worldclock/australia

> **IMPORTANT:**
>
> Each state has different time zone rule. QLD, SA and WA are on a different time zone from NSW, ACT and VIC.

Chapter 4 – Reference links

100 points of ID

- *https://www.afp.gov.au/sites/default/files/PDF/NPC-100PointChecklist-18042019.pdf*

- *www.sydneymovingguide.com/100-points-id/*

Photo Card/ID

- *www.service.nsw.gov.au/transaction/apply-for-a-nsw-photo-card*.

Road rule guides – Car

- *www.nsw.gov.au/driving-boating-and-transport/driver-and-rider-licences/licence-publications*

Road rule guides - Motorcycle

- *www.nsw.gov.au/sites/default/files/2021-05/motorcycle-riders-handbook.pdf*

Driving test guide & fee

- *www.nsw.gov.au/sites/default/files/2021-08/guide-to-driving-test.pdf*

- *www.nsw.gov.au/driving-boating-and-transport/driver-and-rider-licences/fees*

Transferring an overseas driver licence

- *www.nsw.gov.au/driving-boating-and-transport/driver-and-rider-licences/visiting-or-moving-to-nsw*

- *www.nsw.gov.au/driving-boating-and-transport/driver-and-rider-licences/visiting-or-moving-to-nsw/moving-your-overseas-licence/knowledge-and-driving-test-exemptions*

Renting Properties Search Site

- *www.domain.com.au*

- *www.realestate.com.au*

How does Rental works and obligations

- *www.nsw.gov.au/housing-and-construction/renting-a-place-to-live/renting-a-property-nsw/starting-a-lease/paying-a-rental-bond*

- *www.fairtrading.nsw.gov.au/housing-and-property/renting/rental-bonds-online*

- *www.fairtrading.nsw.gov.au/housing-and-property/renting/starting-a-tenancy*

Calculate your LMI

- *www.loancalculatoraustralia.com.au/lenders-mortgage-insurance-calculator*

Calculate Stamp Duty

- *www.apps09.revenue.nsw.gov.au/erevenue/calculators/fhba.php*

Temporary Resident property purchase surcharge

- *www.revenue.nsw.gov.au/taxes-duties-levies-royalties/transfer-duty/surcharge-purchaser-duty/surcharge-for-individuals*

Foreign Investment Review Board guide

- *https://firb.gov.au/sites/firb.gov.au/files/guidance-notes/02_GN_FIRB.pdf*

Mortgage associated fees

- *www.mortgagechoice.com.au*

Electricity and Gas plans comparison

- *www.energymadeeasy.gov.au*

Self Storage

- *www.kss.com.au*

Consumer Law

- *https://consumer.gov.au/resources-and-guides*

Second-hand market

- *www.gumtree.com.au*

- *www.facebook.com/marketplace/*

Outsource tasks – pick and delivery

- *www.airtasker.com/au/*

National parks in NSW & fees

- *www.nationalparks.nsw.gov.au*

- *www.nationalparks.nsw.gov.au/passes-and-fees*

Ambulance

- *www.ambulance.nsw.gov.au/our-services/accounts-and-fees/ambulance-coverage-if-you-are-a-nsw-resident*

Lifetime Health Cover loading (LHC)

- *www.privatehealth.gov.au/health_insurance/surcharges_incentives/lifetime_health_cover.htm*

Medicare levy surcharge

- *www.ato.gov.au/Individuals/Medicare-and-private-health-insurance/Medicare-levy-surcharge/Medicare-levy-surcharge-income,-thresholds-and-rates/*

Health care insurers

- *www.privatehealth.gov.au/dynamic/insurer*

Worker's compensation

- *www.safeworkaustralia.gov.au/workers-compensation*

Daylight savings

- *www.nsw.gov.au/about-nsw/daylight-saving*

- *www.timeanddate.com/worldclock/australia*

Chapter 5 -
Long Term Stay

EARNING MONEY

Search for work

Search for available job from below sites, most popular and widely used by the recruiters to advertise a role from each sector.

Private Sector - Professional works for corporates

- www.linkedin.com
- www.seek.com
- www.indeed.com

Public Sector - Government

Federal government commonwealth level

- www.directory.gov.au/departments-and-agencies
- www.apsjobs.gov.au/s/

State government NSW level

- www.service.nsw.gov.au/nswgovdirectory

Local government NSW – council level

- www.careersatcouncil.com.au/jobs/

Defence

- www.defence.gov.au/jobs-careers

Defence concerns national security, therefore unless you are already an Australia Citizen, or about to become Citizen from PR visa holding, you can not apply for the role. For more detail www.adfcareers.gov.au/joining/can-i-join/citizenship

Job recruitment agency

- Randstad www.randstad.com.au
- Hays www.hays.com.au
- Adecco www.adecco.com.au
- Morgan McKinley www.morganmckinley.com
- Michael Page www.michaelpage.com.au
- Robert Half www.roberthalf.com.au
- Robert Walters Australia www.robertwalters.com.au
- Six Degrees www.sixdegreesexecutive.com.au

And there are certain agencies offers specialised area of recruitment service if you have a niche skills or experiences focused in specific areas to offer.

Casual and part time work

Depending on your time and availability, casual or part time works are good options to earn money initially.

> **TIP:** Local café and restaurants, shops always post on their wall if they are hiring. Bring your resume along the walk for searching for the post and apply with resume on the spot.

Alternatively, you can visit individual company sites which tends to have more offering of shop staff roles with part time or casual in nature.

Woolworths group
www.wowcareers.com.au/page/Careers/Supermarkets/

Coles
https://colescareers.com.au/au/en/search-results

Kmart, Target
https://jobs.kmart.com.au

Aldi
www.aldicareers.com.au/Jobs

IGA
www.iga.com.au/careers/

Companies such as Airtasker (www.airtasker.com/au/), Event Workforce (https://sparkeventgroup.com/careers/) and Sidekicker (https://sidekicker.com/au/work/) are great way to offer service at your own time to give a hand and earn side money.

> **TIP:** If you enjoy riding and have a bicycle, consider food delivery options such as Pizza Hut, Dominos, Uber Eats and Menulog.

For broader search, visit

- https://au.jora.com
- www.linkedin.com
- www.seek.com
- www.indeed.com

Industry Professional Associations

If you are interested in becoming a member in a particular industry, visit www.sydney.edu.au/careers/students/career-advice-and-development/professional-associations.html and become an associated member.

How to get employed

Overall approach to hiring a candidate

In Australia, it is common that years of local experiences overrides the qualification except for the entry level works. In most of case, even entry level work, employers prefer those with hands on work experience (even it may be working at a cafe or a shop, or volunteering).

Referees

Which brings an important aspect of referees. Towards the end of the job search and application stage, you need to provide at least 2 referees of your previous work relationship. This is evidence of your work ethics and behaviours.

How to get your first job

As Australia prefers local experience over everything else, you might start think how I can even start land on the first job. This can be tricky for many people especially coming as a migrant. Make sure to knock on every possible door to

> **IMPORTANT:**
>
> Don't expect that you will get job easily due to your academic background or years of work experience from where you have migrated from, unless you are applying for a very senior position consciously hiring people having international experiences. You need to be prepared that you are starting almost from beginning to build your local Australian work experience.

What are your rights?

Act and regulation

In NSW, workers (employees, in relation to their employment) are protected by the Fair Work Act 2009 and Work Health and Safety Act 2011.

> **IMPORTANT:**
>
> Visa holders and migrant workers have the same workplace entitlements and protections as all other employees in Australia, regardless of their migration status. Employers engaging foreign workers must ensure that they comply with both Australian workplace laws and immigration laws.

As you will be likely be coming Australia with a visa, know that your work right is equally protected as PR visa holders as well as Citizens.

Refer to Visa Protections – The Assurance Protocol:
www.fairwork.gov.au/find-help-for/visa-holders-migrants/visa-protections-the-assurance-protocol

> **IMPORTANT:**
>
> Do not tolerate or accept your employer's exploitation with your visa condition. Your employer can't cancel your visa, even if you've breached your visa conditions. Only Home Affairs can grant, refuse or cancel visas.

What are some signs of workplace exploitation?

Immigration Home affairs has outlined the possible workplace exploitation against people holds visa:

https://immi.homeaffairs.gov.au/visas/working-in-australia/work-rights-and-exploitation

There are different forms of workplace exploitation. There are also other issues that visa holders may experience.

These include:

- threats to cancel your visa
- wage underpayments
- unfair deductions, deposits or 'cash-back' schemes
- not receiving workplace entitlements, for example, paid leave or superannuation
- having your passport taken and held by someone else
- pressured or made to work beyond the restrictions of a visa
- being pressured to pay an up-front payment or 'deposit' for a job
- employers avoiding paying tax by making cash payments of wages to you
- unpaid training
- being classified as an independent contractor instead of an employee
- unfair deductions from wages for accommodation, training, food or transport.

TIP: If you're a visa holder working in Australia and you're experiencing workplace exploitation you should ask for help from the FWO (Fair Work Ombudsman).

List of worker's rights

Minimum Wage: Employees in NSW have the right to receive at least the minimum wage as set by the Fair Work Commission.

Safe Workplace: Employers must provide a safe and healthy work environment, adhering to occupational health and safety regulations.

Anti-Discrimination: Employees have the right to be free from discrimination based on age, race, gender, disability, religion, sexual orientation, or other protected characteristics.

Privacy: Employees have the right to privacy in their personal information and communications within the workplace.

Freedom of Speech: Employees have the right to express their opinions and engage in political activities outside of work without facing discrimination.

Rest and Meal Breaks: Employees are entitled to rest and meal breaks based on the hours worked, as specified in the applicable awards or agreements.

Parental Leave: Eligible employees have the right to take parental leave for the birth or adoption of a child, as per the National Employment Standards (NES).

Personal/Carer's Leave and Compassionate Leave: Employees are entitled to personal/carer's leave for illness or caring responsibilities and compassionate leave for family emergencies, as per the NES.

Annual Leave: Employees have the right to paid annual leave, which accumulates based on the length of service, as per the NES.

Long Service Leave: After a qualifying period, employees in NSW are entitled to long service leave, which allows for an extended period of paid leave.

Union Rights: Employees have the right to join or not join a union, and employers must not discriminate against employees based on union membership.

Termination and Unfair Dismissal: Employees have the right to fair termination procedures and can seek recourse for unfair dismissal through the Fair Work Commission.

Flexible Work Arrangements: Some employees have the right to request flexible work arrangements, such as part-time or remote work, to help balance work and family commitments.

Anti-Bullying and Harassment: Employees have the right to work in an environment free from bullying, harassment, or discrimination.

Whistle-blower Protections: Employees are protected if they report illegal or unethical conduct in the workplace, and employers must not retaliate against whistle-blowers.

These are not exhaustive list to your right, yet it is what will be considered as the top most important rights as a birthright for any individual who holds right to work in Australia (i.e., tourist visa holders will not be protected for working).

Worker's Right - Resources

Fair Work Resources

www.fairwork.gov.au/tools-and-resources/fact-sheets/rights-and-obligations/protections-at-work#overview

Safe Work NSW Resources – in English and other languages

www.safework.nsw.gov.au/resource-library/the-basics-your-rights-at-work

Safe Work NSW Resource – by Industry

www.safework.nsw.gov.au/your-industry

Safe Work NSW - Health and Safety

www.safework.nsw.gov.au/safety-starts-here/safety-support/your-rights-and-responsibilities-for-health-and-safety/worker-health-and-safety-rights-and-responsibilities

Fair Work - Rights and Obligations Fact Sheets

www.fairwork.gov.au/tools-and-resources/fact-sheets/rights-and-obligations

Superannuation

In Australia, there is a mandatory policy requiring salary earned from working for an employer to be set aside for your retirement fund. This is called Superannuation ('Super') in Australia which is different from pension. Currently Australia's minimum % of mandated superannuation is 11% of taxable income which benefits many of us working class employees. There are some organisations will give higher superannuation (i.e., around ~17.5% is usually offered by the government sector jobs) which is a great benefit.

TIP: Check your employment contract's method of calculation for Super. The most straightforward and transparent method is to give and add Super based on your taxable income (which is also referred as 'base income'). On the other hand, Super can be worked out as part of 'total package'. Usually what this means is Super is not calculated on top of your salary, rather it is factored in as part of your salary. Try to avoid this kind of arrangement as this makes it seems the benefit appears to be greater than what it is.

Superannuation guarantee

Fair Work guides to employer that Super is a mandate, under the Superannuation guarantee:
www.fairwork.gov.au/pay-and-wages/tax-and-superannuation

Under the superannuation guarantee, employers must pay superannuation contributions of 11% of an employee's ordinary time earnings when an employee is:

- over 18 years, or
- under 18 years and works over 30 hours a week.

If eligible, the super guarantee applies to all types of employees including:

- full-time employees
- part-time employees
- casual employees.
- Temporary residents are also eligible for super.

Super must be paid at least every 3 months and into the employee's nominated account.

Who are exempted from superannuation guarantee?

Self-employed

If you're self-employed as a sole trader or in a partnership, you do not have to pay super guarantee for yourself.

High income earners

If you are working for multiple employers, and you have right to be exempted after your 2nd employer receives certificate to exempt you from it.

The only reason behind this is due to maximum cap of super contribution each financial year.

IMPORTANT:

Contributing more than the caps to your super may mean having to pay extra tax.

If you are a very high-income earner, benefit can be rearranged or negotiated with employers so that you can be compensated differently (i.e., receive salary instead).

Superannuation cap - for financial year 2023
- Concessional cap (15% tax benefit) is: $27,500 AUD
- Non – concessional cap (no tax benefit) is: $110,000 AUD

Refer to following reference regarding super rates and thresholds: www.ato.gov.au/Rates/Key-superannuation-rates-and-thresholds

---

IMPORTANT:

Cash payment jobs are subject to superannuation. However, most likely you would find yourself not getting any benefit of receiving superannuation if you decided to work for cash payment work.

These jobs are usually run by an individual for doing a small works such as giving a tuition or working for a shop where employer is only willing to pay wage in cash. Best to avoid the work unless you are ok to not receive superannuation for a short period of time.

Where to store your super

By law, you have right to choose your own superannuation fund. Most of the time, when you join a new company, they will give you an option either to sign up with their nominated super fund or ask you to find your own.

> TIP: It is not a bad idea to go with your own after doing some research. Find the best performing super fund and each time when you move your job, consolidate your super account to one so that you can easily monitor and track them. In the long run, this will save you management fee which gets charged by the super fund.

Refer to best performing super funds:

www.superguide.com.au/comparing-super-funds/best-performing-super-funds

SMSF – self managed super fund

A self-managed super fund (SMSF) is an alternate to retail or industry super fund. A SMSF is a private super fund that you manage yourself.

> TIP: It is easier and more manageable to go with Industry or retail super funds. SMSF, however, can be an attractive option in a longer run for those who are competent in the responsibilities and financially and legally savvy individual.

Check benefits and risk of running your own SMSF:

https://moneysmart.gov.au/how-super-works/self-managed-super-fund-smsf

SETTING UP A BUSINESS

Another way of making your living is by running your own business. Australia is one of the greatest places in the world to set up a business as there are low corruption and bribery. Australia has governing bodies to watch corruptions. Your hard work and skills can't easily be influenced over by unfair power.

ABN, ACN

In Australia, you will require to register ABN for all businesses (including contractors) and ACN for all companies.

Refer to: https://squareup.com/au/en/townsquare/difference-between-abn-and-acn

Hobby vs Business

If you consider your earning as a hobby, you do not require ABN. Please check how it compares:
https://business.gov.au/planning/new-businesses/difference-between-a-business-and-a-hobby

Eligibility

Generally, you can set up business as without being a permanent resident or Citizen. Make sure to check your eligibility here: https://business.gov.au/planning/new-businesses/start-a-business-as-a-non-citizen

> **IMPORTANT:**
>
> Check for any restriction on your visa to set up a business.

ASIC – Australian Securities and Investments Commission

In Australia, ASIC regulates the conduct of Australian companies, financial markets, financial services organisations.

Find more information provided by ASIC here: https://asic.gov.au/for-business/small-business/starting-a-small-business/

Ready to start your business

If you have checked all the points above and if you are ready to set up your business, refer to the guide regarding each steps to successfully setup your business here: https://business.gov.au/guide/starting

REALLY IMPORTANT THINGS TO NOTE - AT ANY MOMENT

Scam & Fraud

Scam in Australia is increasing day by day, and it is a serious threat to many individuals as well as to the entire nation's economy. The money that has been scammed and lost due to scammers in Australia in year 2022 is $3.1 billion AUD.

Scammers tend to target the most vulnerable people especially - by their relationship status, visa status or even social background status (i.e., immigrants with very less understanding or familiarity of services and products available in Australia).

Scammers knows how to exploit trends or hot topics that triggers people mind which are cared by many people during the crime. Scammers can play with mind of those who are most vulnerable - especially people who are on a visa.

Following is a good reference guide that can help you be more aware and prevent yourself falling as a victim of a scam.

Detect scammer's website
www.scam-detector.com

Australian Scam watch reporting site
www.scamwatch.gov.au

Protect from Scam guide
www.accc.gov.au/consumers/protecting-yourself/scams

Scammer's tactic to watch out for year 2023
www.aarp.org/money/scams-fraud/info-2023/top-scammer-tactics-2023.html

Companies you should not deal with
https://moneysmart.gov.au/companies-you-should-not-deal-with

Chapter 5 – Reference links

Job Search sites

- *www.linkedin.com*

- *www.seek.com*

- *www.indeed.com*

- *www.directory.gov.au/departments-and-agencies*

- *www.apsjobs.gov.au/s/*

- *www.service.nsw.gov.au/nswgovdirectory*

- *www.careersatcouncil.com.au/jobs/*

- *www.defence.gov.au/jobs-careers*

- *www.adfcareers.gov.au/joining/can-i-join/citizenship*

- *www.randstad.com.au*

- *www.hays.com.au*

- *www.adecco.com.au*

- *www.morganmckinley.com*

- *www.michaelpage.com.au*

- *www.roberthalf.com.au*

- *www.robertwalters.com.au*

- *www.sixdegreesexecutive.com.au*

- *www.wowcareers.com.au/page/Careers/Supermarkets/*

- *https://colescareers.com.au/au/en/search-results*

- *https://jobs.kmart.com.au*

- *www.aldicareers.com.au/Jobs*

- *www.iga.com.au/careers/*

- *www.airtasker.com/au/*

- *https://sparkeventgroup.com/careers/*

- *https://sidekicker.com/au/work/*

- *www.uber.com/au/en/e/deliver/*

- *https://couriers.menulog.com.au/application/*

- *https://au.jora.com*

Industry Professional Associations

- *www.sydney.edu.au/careers/students/career-advice-and-development/professional-associations.html*

Worker's right

- *www.fairwork.gov.au/find-help-for/visa-holders-migrants/visa-protections-the-assurance-protocol*

- *https://immi.homeaffairs.gov.au/visas/working-in-australia/work-rights-and-exploitation*

- *www.fairwork.gov.au/tools-and-resources/fact-sheets/rights-and-obligations/protections-at-work#overview*

- *www.safework.nsw.gov.au/resource-library/the-basics-your-rights-at-work*

- *www.safework.nsw.gov.au/your-industry*

- *www.safework.nsw.gov.au/safety-starts-here/safety-support/your-rights-and-responsibilities-for-health-and-safety/worker-health-and-safety-rights-and-responsibilities*

- *www.fairwork.gov.au/tools-and-resources/fact-sheets/rights-and-obligations*

Superannuation

- *www.fairwork.gov.au/pay-and-wages/tax-and-superannuation*

- *www.ato.gov.au/Rates/Key-superannuation-rates-and-thresholds*

- *www.superguide.com.au/comparing-super-funds/best-performing-super-funds*

- *https://moneysmart.gov.au/how-super-works/self-managed-super-fund-smsf*

Setting up a business

- *https://squareup.com/au/en/townsquare/difference-between-abn-and-acn*

- *https://business.gov.au/planning/new-businesses/difference-between-a-business-and-a-hobby*

- *https://business.gov.au/planning/new-businesses/start-a-business-as-a-non-citizen*

- *https://asic.gov.au/for-business/small-business/starting-a-small-business/*

- *https://business.gov.au/guide/starting*

Scam and Fraud how to watch out

- *www.scam-detector.com*

- *www.scamwatch.gov.au*

- *www.accc.gov.au/consumers/protecting-yourself/scams*

- *www.aarp.org/money/scams-fraud/info-2023/top-scammer-tactics-2023.html*

- *https://moneysmart.gov.au/companies-you-should-not-deal-with*

INDEX

ABOUT THE AUTHOR

 Meet Soo and Biswanath, two individuals who have embarked on unique paths as immigrants to Australia. Through their experiences, they have gained profound insights into the challenges and opportunities of settling in a new country.

Soo left her homeland of South Korea during her teenage years in the year 2000, venturing to Australia for high school. On the other hand, Biswanath pursued his master's degree in Australia after coming from India, delving into various professional roles including software engineering.

Despite their different backgrounds, Biswanath and Soo share a common passion for assisting others in navigating the complexities of migration. With a wealth of personal stories, tips, and guidance, they aim to make the migration experience smoother for fellow immigrants.

Printed in Great Britain
by Amazon

45579373R00069